Guide for TUTORS

Mark L. Greenwood

Dionysus Publishing

Greenwood's Guide for Tutors, 1st edition, Improve your skills and excel in the world of tutoring.

For information, address Dionysus Publishing, 3656 Williams Avenue, Claremont, California 91711. First Printing 2003. Printed and bound in The United States of America.

ISBN: 1-932345-01-9

LCCN: 2003090328

Acknowledgments

Many thanks to Dr. Frank Torres of California Polytechnic University, Pomona, for giving me the opportunity to put together a training program for his tutors. It was Dr. Torres' vision for a certified tutor training program, along with his full support of my efforts, that made this book possible.

Preface

I've been involved in tutoring, at various levels, for more than twenty years, and I am still hard pressed to find a more rewarding and exciting activity. Very little can compete with the satisfaction you get when something "clicks" and a tutee suddenly understands a concept for the first time.

This kind of success is one of the major rewards of being a tutor...But it doesn't happen automatically. Good tutoring is a by-product of experience and training. This book was put together to give both new and seasoned tutors the tools that they need to succeed in the world of tutoring. It contains practical, hands-on information that can be put to work by you to get the most out of your tutoring sessions.

This book came about through my efforts to establish a certified tutor training program at California State Polytechnic University, Pomona. Finding very little in the way of practical material on the market, I started attending a variety of educational conferences. Information gathered from these conferences, along with years of experience and invaluable input from tutors, led to our tutor training program and ultimately this book.

I hope that you enjoy reading this book as much as I enjoyed writing it, and I wish you much success as a tutor.

About the Author

I had my first taste of tutoring back in 1972 when I took a student job as a tutor in the mathematics department. I realized right then and there that I enjoyed sharing my knowledge of math with others. I also began to realize the influence that tutoring could have on a person's academic success. A few years later after graduating with a BS in math, I faced one of my greatest tutoring challenges: home-schooling my daughter, Jeni. For nine years I tutored Jeni in a variety of subjects and grade levels. At age sixteen, she attended her first college class, and I was happy to see the positive benefits that my tutoring experience had yielded. She is now pursuing her Ph.D. in history. During those nine years of tutoring, I discovered that communication and coaching were far more important than an advanced knowledge of the subject matter.

During the home-schooling years, and with a lot of coaxing from my wife, I went back to school and obtained an MS in math, which led to a part-time teaching position at a local college. As an instructor, I gained a whole new appreciation and understanding of tutoring and the differences between the classroom and the tutoring environment. As luck would have it, I was also offered a position at the Learning Resource Center at a local university. I was given the opportunity not only to coordinate their math preparation program, but also to develop a comprehensive tutor training program. Being an applied mathematician, I was looking for practical material to share with my tutors. My search for training materials was discouraging. Most of what I found was too theoretical to be of much use to my tutor trainees or me. So I followed in the footsteps of other tutor trainers.

I attended many conferences: ACCTLA (Association for California College Tutorial and Learning Assistance), CRLA (College Reading & Learning Association), and WESTOP (Western Association of Educational Opportunity Personnel). I collected every handout I could get my hands on. I then compiled my own tutor training program from these handouts. After a short while, I had also compiled information and experience from nearly every angle of the tutoring world: tutor, tutee, teacher, tutor trainer, tutor coordinator. Greenwood's Guide for Tutors is the collection of all of those invaluable years of experience.

My tutor training program had its official debut in the fall of 1995, and was certified the following winter. Today, the training program bears little resemblance to that stack of papers and handouts that started it all back in 1995. It has taken a much more hands-on approach, and the subject matter itself has been simultaneously broadened and deepened. One rewarding aspect, among many, is that the tutors enjoy the more hands-on flavor that the program has taken. It was this practical approach to tutoring and the positive response from my tutors, that led me to author this book.

Table of Contents

Introduction

How To Use This Book

Tutors, both new and experienced, can benefit from this book. Take, for example, session dynamics. It is an unfortunate fact that many tutors do too much of the talking and too much of the work during the tutoring session. This book is full of suggestions for getting the tutee more involved.

Instructors can gain a new appreciation of tutoring dynamics, as well. Some of the suggested techniques may even be used to improve time spent after class (or during office hours) with students.

Tutor trainers can build their program around this book. It provides the general tutoring techniques needed by all tutors, regardless of the subjects or student levels they tutor. The role playing exercises present invaluable suggestions for assessing the tutor's understanding of the techniques, while at the same time, generating discussions and ideas for improvement.

This book basically follows the logical tutoring sequence: set-up, greeting, starting a session, tutoring, ending a session. Therefore it is best to read beginning to end without jumping around. Scattered throughout the book are exercises. They can be approached in three different ways, depending on your tutoring environment.

Option 1: In a classroom, or group training environment, the scenarios can be role-played by two participants. Role playing has two main benefits. One, it allows participants to demonstrate their understanding of the material by acting out solutions. Two, non-participants learn by observation and can provide critical input. It is often valuable to role-play the scenario twice: once doing things the "wrong" way and once, the "right" way. Not only does this approach better demonstrate the benefits of good tutoring ideas, but it is also a lot more fun!

Option 2: In a classroom, one-on-one, or individual environment, the scenarios can be addressed through the writing of a short paper. Addressing a scenario on paper forces you to think about the material and apply what you have learned to a possible situation before it comes up in an actual tutoring session.

Option 3: In a classroom or one-on-one environment, the tutor trainer may want to get verbal responses to the scenarios. This may be used by a tutor trainer to obtain a quick assessment as to the readiness of a new tutor. In a classroom situation, verbal responses could be used to spur discussion and generate new ideas.

Practice Makes Perfect!

Practice makes perfect! Near the end of this book is a list of additional scenarios that can be role-played, or practiced with a friend. These offer helpful ways to 'get your feet wet' before sitting down with a tutee.

Chapter 1

The Perfect Setting

Suppose you are meeting a client for lunch to go over some figures or look over a sales report. First, the waitress seats you at a small table for two. No problem...after all, there are only two of you eating, right? When the water arrives, things are a little cramped, but it still looks like you'll have plenty of workspace. By the time you both get your coffee, sandwiches, cream for the coffee, silverware...

You get the picture!

There is barely any room left to eat, and even less room for paperwork. In addition to the poor lighting conditions of the restaurant, there

Key Concepts!

- Choose a spacious work environment
- Sit beside your tutee
- Find a quiet, well-lit work area
- No food or drinks!

is a loud, boisterous gentleman seated at the table beside yours. As he begins to enthusiastically act out a story, he pauses to light up a cigar. So far, this is not turning out to be a very suitable environment for going over complex figures. To make matters worse, you are seated opposite your client, which makes it nearly impossible to review the same papers. To top off this unproductive meeting, your client spills coffee all over the papers.

It's a safe bet that not much work got done during this meeting.

A proper tutoring environment is very important, and it is your responsibility to provide it. The environment in which the tutoring takes place can mean the difference between success and failure. And although you may be required to use a tutoring center's facilities, there are still some things you can do to create the perfect tutoring environment.

Choosing A Table

Choose a table (if possible) that is large enough to accommodate all the materials that you and your tutee will be using during your session. If you are forced to use a smaller table, place materials immediately required on the table while storing those that will be needed later in an easily accessible place, such as on the floor next to your chair. It is also important to choose a table that allows side-by-side seating; this will provide both you and your tutee with a clear view of the material. There are no formal rules about which side of your tutee you should be seated on, but I prefer to sit on my writing side. For example, I am right handed, so I always sit to my tutee's right; if you are left handed, you may wish to be seated to your tutee's left. This arrangement keeps the tutor's writing hand away from the tutee, making it more difficult for the tutor to reach in and take over the tutee's work (see the section about doing your tutee's work). Choose a table, whenever possible, that offers quiet surroundings, minimal distractions, ample lighting, fresh air, and comfortable temperature. A tutee who is distracted by unfavorable conditions will not be 100 percent focused on the session. And a lack of focus can be detrimental to both learning and information retention.

An exception to the above is group tutoring. Group tutoring requires an environment that allows the tutor to act as a facilitator for the entire group while, at the same time, allowing individual tutees to interact with one another. A large, round table often works well for group tutoring sessions. They allow plenty of workspace, while allowing everyone to interact face-to-face.

No Food or Drink

You're running late for your next tutoring session and there's no time to stop for lunch. So you decide to pick up a mega burrito, with extra hot sauce, and a large coffee, and take them to the session. You plop down the burrito and tear off the lid from the paper cup. You're just washing down the first bite of burrito with a mouthful of strong, black coffee when your tutee arrives.

What's wrong with this picture? Everything!

One - your breath is most likely lethal. The hot-sauce-coffee breath...it's not a pleasant odor. It's difficult for a tutee to give full attention to the session when he or she is preoccupied with trying to avoid your breath.

Two - Are you really going to give 100 percent of your attention and effort to the session while you're eating your lunch? Doubtful!

Three - What if your tutee hasn't had lunch? Imagine you're hungry, and you have to spend the next hour watching someone else eat their lunch. As your stomach growls, and your mouth waters, your focus would probably be on the food and not on the work.

Four - The burrito, paper wrapper, and coffee cup are making it difficult to access necessary materials on the table. Suppose you reach for a piece of paper and accidentally dump the entire cup of coffee on your tutee's work. Not just any piece of work, a ten-page, typed, masterpiece that took two weeks to put together. All ten pages are soaked with coffee. Is your tutee upset? Definitely.

For all of the above reasons, I strongly recommend that dining not be a part of your tutoring experience.

Exercise

The Hungry Tutee

Your tutee arrives with half a sandwich and a can of soda. How would you handle this situation?

Chapter 2

Keep it Clean, Folks!

Personal Hygiene

There is nothing more distracting than sitting next to someone who has just finished a good workout and didn't have time to shower before the tutoring session.

We're talking Big Time B.O. here!

Key Concepts!

- Good hygiene is more appreciated than you may think
- Fresh breath can prevent embarrassing distractions
- Appropriate attire can impact your tutoring session

This type of distraction takes away from concentration, and thus, learning ability is greatly decreased. And yet, this type of distraction is really easy to remedy. A quick shower or a little deodorant goes a long way in the world of tutoring; and it really helps to keep your tutee focused on the session instead of on your lack of personal hygiene. The key word in all of this, however, is Little...as in a Little cologne or perfume.

Don't go overboard!

Ever ride in an elevator with a woman who reeks of cheap perfume or a man who has drenched himself in cologne? It is distracting in an elevator, so you can imagine how distracting it could be during a tutoring session. If you splash on too much perfume or cologne, it will most likely become very distracting to the tutee.

You should also consider your breath, particularly if you are a smoker or a heavy coffee drinker. I'm a coffee drinker, and I once had a lady offer me a mint during one of our tutoring sessions. I wasn't sure if she was just offering, or if my breath was aggravating her; I'll never know for sure. But one thing I do know, I always chew a stick of gum or have a mint handy prior to a tutoring session.

Dress For Tutoring

The old saying is true...
"You can't judge a book by its cover."

But, there are some scenarios when a person's clothes can be so distracting or disturbing that it makes a tutoring session difficult, if not impossible. Let's say, for example, that a female tutor comes to a session dressed in a bikini top and hot pants; she's probably going to have a difficult time getting her male tutee to pay attention to their work and not her outfit. The same is true for male tutors. If a male tutor shows up to a session wearing a stained, sweaty muscle T-shirt and a pair of hot pink bicycle shorts, it's going to be difficult not to focus on his attire. Besides the fact that it is distracting, improper attire can also damage the credibility of the tutor. Without a doubt, improper clothing can have a negative effect on your entire tutoring session. On the other hand, as a tutor, you can also be TOO formal or professional in your dress; especially if you're a peer tutor. If you show up to the tutoring session in a business suit, you run the risk of intimidating your tutee.

Exercise

Late

Gym class ran late. You now have two choices: do a quick change of clothes and make it on time to your tutoring session; take a shower and be a bit late. Which would you choose and why?

Another problem is attire that is socially inappropriate or offensive. Jokes, slogans, and radical group affiliations printed across clothing are all distractions that could offend your tutee and negatively impact your time together.

As a tutor, this is easy to remedy; don't wear anything that could be considered offensive by your tutee. For example, a tutee came into my office a few years ago with a complaint; his tutor was wearing a shirt that had several offensive "jokes" printed across the front and back. Good judgement and common sense could have prevented this awkward situation.

If you find yourself with a tutee who exhibits offensive behavior via clothing, it is best to discuss it with your supervisor or another authority figure within the tutoring center, and let them confront the tutee.

If your center has a dress code for tutees, you should make it known to your tutee during your first meeting together (see Reviewing Rules and Other Information, Chapter 4).

Chapter 3

A Crash Course in Diversity

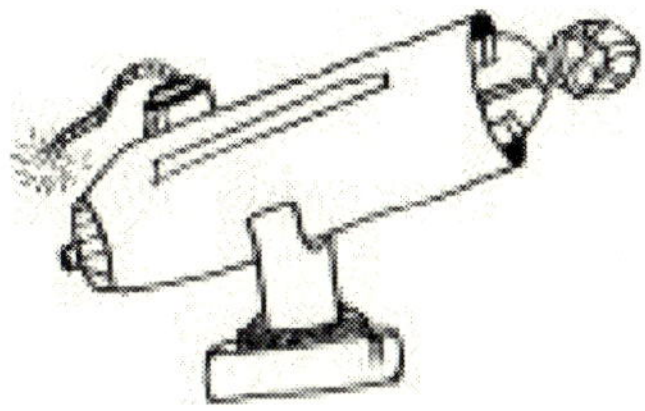

DIVERSITY MEANS DIFFERENT

Diversity is the condition of being different. Yes, a diverse tutee could be a person who is of another culture...but how about a different race, gender, or religion? These could include people who are physically challenged, people with mental disabilities, albinos, those born with dwarfism...

You get the idea!

Consider a professional working as a loan officer at a local banking institution. The loan officer helps a variety of different people every day. Yet, a very similar approach is utilized with each new client. Most likely a handshake, followed by a "Hi, how may I help you today?" It's safe to assume that the loan officer will not extend a high-five to a client and greet him with a "How's it going, Man?" based on the fact that the potential customer has a beard and drove up to the bank in a brightly colored van. The loan officer is expected to treat each client with complete respect, whether that client is a young woman in a pair of jeans and a t-shirt, or an older gentleman wearing a tuxedo. Tutors are expected to do the same; treat each person fairly no matter how unusual the tutee might seem. It is also important to realize that differences usually seem more vast than they really are. For example, a 60 year old woman may appear to have little in common with a 19 year old man until they begin getting to know one another. Suddenly, both discover that they share a love of mathematics, and coffee. These common interests not only dispel the notion that these two different individuals have nothing in common, but they have also proven that people are often more alike than they realize.

Key Concepts!

- Diversity is more than just cultural
- Don't stereotype
- Treat every tutee with respect
- Be polite and professional

As a tutor, you are not expected to know everything about diversity. There are thousands of books on the subject and many of them don't agree with each other. The bottom line is that every person is a unique individual, so don't generalize or stereotype. Instead, use a standard, professional approach with all of your tutees. Then adjust the manner in which you interact as you get to know your tutee as an individual. Treat all of your tutees with the respect that every human being deserves. And if something is still on your mind, don't assume, stereotype, or stare...ASK! People are usually glad to interact if they are sincerely approached.

Chapter 4

Greet That Tutee!

Greetings are an important part of a tutoring session, and each greeting will differ depending upon how well you know your tutee.

Consider a host greeting guests as they arrive at his party. “Nice to see you, Doris,” the host says as he hugs Doris. “Bob, you old son-of-a-gun! How’s that new job working out?” asks the host, vigorously shaking Bob’s hand. “Hello, I’m your host, Gerry. Pleased to meet you.” The host (Gerry) doesn’t use the exact same greeting for every guest arriving at his party. Some guests, like Doris, require a brief, but friendly acknowledgment.

Key Concepts!

- Greetings will vary based on familiarity
- Friendly conversation creates a comfortable environment
- Let your tutee know the rules up front

Other guests, such as Bob, need more personal attention. Still other guests are new to Gerry, and they require a more formal greeting and a full introduction. However, regardless of who the guest is, or how well the host knows them, it is Gerry's job to make each person feel welcome and comfortable.

The same is true of tutoring, it is your job to make each tutee with whom you work feel comfortable. Greetings and introductions are an excellent way to accomplish this. As illustrated above, your greeting will vary from person to person, particularly in the case of a new tutee. After a short while, the various types of greetings, and their intended uses, will come naturally to you. Just as our party host knew instinctively how to greet each guest, so too will you instinctively know how to greet your tutees.

Greeting Tutees You've Tutored Before

A simple, "Hello" followed by a little personal chit-chat is about all that is required before getting to work with a tutee whom you have tutored before. Keep the personal conversation to a minimum, but be friendly and talkative enough to make your tutee feel comfortable. Keep in mind, however, that the average length of a tutoring session is only about an hour; it would not be fair to the tutee to use the entire session time with a personal conversation.

Greeting New Tutees

If this is your first time with the tutee, you should start with an introduction. Tell your tutee a little bit about yourself. Mention your major, hobbies, interests, and anything else that could help your tutee get to know you as a person. This kind of information will make your tutee more comfortable and better able to relate to you.

Likewise, find out about your tutee's interests, hobbies, etc.. Not only will you get to know your tutee better, but often, during a tutoring session, you can relate material directly to your tutee's hobbies and interests. This could make the material much more easily understandable to your tutee. Find out (if applicable) who your tutee's instructor is, and take a look at the class syllabus and text. An instructor can be a valuable source of information, and in some cases can even provide you with a copy of the class text. A class syllabus can often help in planning for future sessions.

Reviewing Rules and Other Information

You've just been pulled over by a police officer, but you are not sure why. "You made a right turn at that intersection," the officer announces, "and there's a 'no right turn on red' at that intersection." You explain to the officer that you didn't see a sign indicating no right turn on red. "Oh," replies the officer, "the sign fell down a couple of months ago, but it was there for over a year. You must have read it."

HELLO! You can't be expected to follow the rules unless you know what they are.

Therefore, when meeting with your tutee for the first time, review all rules pertaining to the tutee: How long will you wait for a late tutee? What happens if the tutee doesn't show up? What is the procedure for rescheduling a session? Don't assume that the tutee has already read (or heard) the rules and understands them. Also, make sure that the tutee has your phone number, as well as any other appropriate phone numbers. In addition, get the tutee's phone number in case you have to reschedule a session.

Exercise

Practicing Your Greeting Skills

You are greeting a new tutee for the first time. What information should you give the tutee? What information should you get from the tutee?

Chapter 5

Goals and Agendas

You meet with your tutee for the very first time. He or she needs help with algebra. You've set up a good environment for tutoring, the introductions have been made, and you've reviewed the rules with your tutee. You've done everything perfectly up to this point. Now you turn to your tutee and say, "Okay, let's start off by simplifying complex fractions." HUH?!?!! Unless you're some kind of a mind reader, how do you know what your tutee needs help with? Maybe your tutee is proficient at complex fractions. Maybe he or she needs help with exponents. Let's assume that you got lucky and your tutee was having

> **Key Concepts!**
>
> - Goals help the tutor establish what needs to get done
> - Goals allow the tutee to get more out of a session
> - Agendas are great for managing a session

problems with complex fractions. Where is the session headed? How are complex fractions going to be addressed? What is missing here is a goal and an agenda.

Your tutee comes to you for help. Your tutee may know exactly where the problem lies, but more often than not, your tutee will be unclear as to where help is actually needed. Your tutee's cry for help can be a specific such as, "I understand everything but this one problem," or as vague as "I don't get this stuff." It's your job, as the tutor, to figure out where help is needed. This can be accomplished by asking questions and listening (see Questioning and Listening, Chapter 5), looking over previous work assignments, or anything else that might help pinpoint where he or she needs help. Once the problem area is identified, a goal needs to be set. A goal can be anything from "I want to learn word problems" to "I want to get a B in this class." The purpose of a goal is to let you know what your tutee wants to accomplish, either during the session, or as a result of many sessions.

In either case, it's your tutee who must decide on a goal. Therefore, let your tutee (with guidance from you) tell you what he or she wants to accomplish. The agenda is your responsibility. As the tutor, you can use your knowledge of the subject to break down problems into a series of small steps that can be mastered one at a time. These steps will form an agenda for the session. Let's say that your tutee is having a problem with fractions. You might respond with "Let's start with the common denominator, then we'll add and subtract fractions, and then we'll review the greatest common factor so that we can reduce fractions."

Keep in mind that this is not a classroom session. You are not required to stick to the agenda and cover a prescribed amount of material during the session. Ultimately, your tutee's pace will drive the session.

So why an agenda?
Here are some convincing reasons.

One, an agenda helps you to break down a task into manageable parts for your tutee. Smaller tasks are much easier to work on.

Two, the agenda lets your tutee see what will be covered and the logical progression.

And last, but certainly not least, it models positive student behavior. This is important because, in addition to direct learning, your tutee will also learn from your actions and vocabulary.

With any luck your tutee will pick up a few helpful habits.

Chapter 6

Verbal Communication Techniques

Communication plays an integral role in every aspect of society and tutoring is no exception. The communication techniques and skills that you demonstrate as a tutor can significantly impact the session.

Communication helps determine what needs to be done, and how it will be accomplished. Communication also plays an important role in creating an environment in which your tutee will never feel embarrassed or "dumb" during a session.

Key Concepts!

- Communication is a two-way street
- Encourage your tutee to talk
- Keep lecturing to a minimum
- Give tutees time to respond

Questioning and Listening

Suppose you go to your family physician with a sore throat. The nurse directs you to a small examining room where you patiently wait for the doctor to arrive.

Suddenly, the doctor bursts into the room and shouts, “Okay, let’s X-ray that leg!” Huh?!? Of course, in reality, this would never happen because doctors are trained to locate a problem before they attempt to fix it. And the most successful technique that the physician employs to locate a problem is to ask the patient.

The doctor in the above example would most likely ask about the patient’s symptoms, medical history, where the pain is located, etc. Once the questions are asked, the doctor would employ another invaluable tool - listening! The physician would not rush in and immediately provide an answer without first listening to you describe your condition yourself. Imagine the

> **Exercise**
>
> ***Lost***
>
> When asked where assistance is needed, your tutee responds, “I don’t understand any of this stuff.” How do you proceed?

doctor asking you, "So, what brought you here?" And before you even have the chance to describe your sore throat, the doctor interrupts with, "I knew it! It's your leg. We need to get that X-rayed, stat!"

By asking the proper questions and listening to your answers, the doctor can determine what needs to be treated (goal) and the treatment process (agenda) that will be utilized.

Tutoring is a similar business. Your tutee comes to you for help. He or she is having some difficulty with a particular subject. Your job, as the tutor, is to figure out what problems need to be addressed. This can be best accomplished through a process of questioning and listening. Ask questions that will reveal where your tutee is at the present time. "Show (or tell) me where you are having difficulty," is a question that will reveal much more than, "So, do you understand this stuff?" Ask questions that require more than a "yes" or "no" response. Your ultimate goal here is to get the tutee to tell you where the help is needed.

The Silent Treatment

Ever hear of something called the "silent treatment"?

That's when you don't talk to someone until they can't stand the silence any longer and they feel compelled to say something. Try it sometime. It really works!

Actually, tutees use the silent treatment on their tutors all the time. Tutees are famous for keeping silent until their tutor answers all of their questions or does all of their work. In too many of the tutoring sessions that I have observed, the tutor does too much talking and the tutee doesn't do enough. The silent treatment should be employed by you, and not your tutee. You should give your tutee ample time to think about a problem or question and respond with an answer. Remember that your tutee may require more time than you would to come up with an answer. So, be patient! But don't be ridiculous with the silence. You can keep silent for the entire session, and it still won't help your tutee come up with a response if he or she lacks the skills or knowledge to do so. Provide a reasonable amount of silence (10-20 seconds) before interjecting with assistance.

Lecturing

Lecturing is something that teachers do, not tutors.

As a general rule, tutors should not lecture. There are times, however, when lecturing can be a valuable tutoring method. Let's say that the silent treatment bears no fruit. A little questioning and listening on your part reveals that your tutee was never exposed to the particular topic or skill needed to solve the problem. Your tutee needs to learn some new material before the session can progress any further.

In this situation, a short lecture is often a very effective way to present new material to your tutee. When using this technique, however, keep the lecturing to a minimum; just enough to introduce the necessary materials. Then use some of the other techniques mentioned in this book to assess your tutee's understanding of the newly learned material.

Exercise

The Quiet, Unmotivated Type

Your tutee is extremely quiet and somewhat unmotivated. How can you improve this situation?

Chapter 7

Written Communication Techniques

"A picture is worth a thousand words!"

This is especially true in the world of tutoring. There are times when explaining something just isn't enough to make the concept completely clear. And there are other times when a quick sketch or a clear example can help bring a complex idea into focus for the tutee.

Diagrams and Drawings

Have you ever had someone "tell" you how to get somewhere? They give you a quick set of directions over the phone, and you end up getting lost.

Key Concepts!

- A picture can be worth a thousand words
- Choose example problems that show exactly what you want
- Demonstrate concepts if necessary

If you're a visual person like me, you'll need a map. Whenever I ask for directions, I always ask the person to draw a map that I can refer to along my route. This allows me to better understand the route that I will need to take, while also giving me something to refer back to whenever I need to.

The same general principle applies to tutoring. When lecturing is not working or is not an appropriate way to present new material, drawings or diagrams may be a wiser choice. Take parabolas, for example. A short lecture might point out that a parabola is a set of points in a plane which are equidistant from a fixed focal point and a fixed line in the plane. This might be a short, accurate lecture, but the image may still be unclear. to the tutee In this case, a simple drawing of a parabola would reveal a lot.

Demonstrations

When surgeons need to learn a new procedure, they attend lectures, read articles, go to professional conferences, and study charts and diagrams. But after all of this intense study and all of this exposure to the procedure, they are still not ready to try it out on their own. Why? Because they need something more. They need a demonstration. By observing other experts demonstrating a new procedure, the surgeons gain a better understanding of how the procedure looks when performed. Only after observing the procedure in action are they ready to try it on their own.

In any tutoring situation, an occasion could arise when lectures, diagrams, or drawings are simply not working; it is also possible that none of these three techniques are appropriate given the subject matter. For these occasions, demonstrations may be what is needed.

Consider an archery class. One of the first steps you need to learn is how to string a bow. Assuming that it is a beginner's class and no one has ever strung a bow, silence will not yield an answer. A short lecture reveals only that the bow must be bent enough to slip on the bowstring. Rather obvious, but how exactly is it done? A drawing simply shows how the bow and bowstring are actually handled during the process. An interesting picture, but it doesn't help much either. Is it a quick bending motion of the bow? Or does a slow bend work? How is the string guided during the procedure? What is needed is a demonstration. You need to SEE HOW to string the bow as it happens. In this case, one demonstration will do what all of the other techniques failed to do -- teach the class how a bow is strung.

Example Problems

Choosing appropriate example problems can also be an important aspect of a successful tutoring session. For example, I once tutored an individual who gave 11 as the answer to the following problem:

$$xx - yy \text{ ; When } x = 6 \text{ and } y = 5$$

In my head, I quickly worked out the problem.

$$6 \times 6 - 5 \times 5 = 36 - 25 = 11$$

"Yup, correct answer," I thought.

So, we moved on...Two sessions later the same problem appeared, but this time it was to be solved for $x = 3$ and $y = 2$.

To my surprise, my tutee came up, once again, with 11 as the answer. "This can't be right," I thought, as I worked out the problem.

$3 \times 3 - 2 \times 2 = 9 - 4$ ... "That's not 11..."

Obviously something was wrong.

I soon discovered that my tutee did not know that there was an implied multiplication between the two variables. My tutee was solving the problem as follows: for $x = 6$ and $y = 5$

$$66 - 55 = 11$$

And for $x = 3$ and $y = 2$, $33 - 22 = 11$

In short, the original problem with $x = 6$ and $y = 5$ was not a good example to use. Had I used $x = 3$ and $y = 2$ for the first example, I would have immediately understood that my tutee had a problem with implied multiplication. Beware of other confusing examples, such as $2^2=4$. If $2^2=4$ then to the unknowing tutee 3^2 might equal 3×2. Always use exampls that clearly demonstrate a concept.

Chapter 8

Working With Your Tutee

Perhaps this section should be titled, "Work With, **Not For**, Your Tutee."

This is one of the most important aspects to emphasize in this section. More than once, I have found a tutor not only doing the work during a session, but also doing the tutee's homework and classwork! And trust me, as you read through this section, you will learn that nothing could be more detrimental to your tutees than not letting them complete their own work.

Don't Do Your Tutee's Work!

Do you want to be a "Super Tutor"? Helping thousands of students...Lounging on a white sandy beach while you count out all of your money made from tutoring? Then, do your tutees' homework! Think about it. You feel good because you "helped" your tutees get all of their work finished. Your tutees are happy because not only is their work completed on time, but their grade is guaranteed to improve. Then there are the bonuses. Your tutees think you are the greatest tutor in existence. And, since your tutees are now totally dependent on your skills to complete the work, you are getting paid for a lot more tutoring sessions!

Sounds like a win-win situation, right?

WRONG!

In reality, that entire scenario is just bad tutoring. It may be a successful business model, but it is an unsuccessful tutoring strategy.

The sign of a truly successful tutor is one who works himself or herself out of a job!

Key Concepts!

- Let your tutees do the work
- Continually assess your tutee's level
- Let your tutees demonstrate what they have learned before moving on

Your goal is to get your tutees to the point where they can perform on their own. That means that they will no longer require your services. Not doing your tutees' work is a great place to start!

Let Your Tutee Do The Work

This is one of the most violated rules in tutoring. One reason is that it seems so much more "efficient" for a tutor to "show" a tutee how to do something. They will learn by pure observation, right? WRONG! While demonstrating a problem is helpful, simply doing every aspect of your tutees' work is not helpful at all. I remember one of my relatives who was brilliant at what he did, but he was a terrible tutor. A typical lesson would go something like this:

He would tell me how to do something.

I would start to perform the task.

He would immediately butt in and "show" me the exact (proper) way to do it

End of lesson

After a few months, I was well trained at how to watch someone else perform a task. In fact, I became conditioned to hesitate until he showed me how to do something. That way, I wouldn't have to be reminded that I wasn't doing it correctly. Unfortunately, this made it difficult to learn anything. And, after every session, I was still lacking the skills that I had been attempting to acquire. There is great value in doing things for yourself, and this is true in the tutoring environment, as well.

The act of "doing" reinforces learning, and an excellent way to get your tutee to do the work is to give him or her control of the materials. And that includes the pen or pencil! I admit it, I still grab the pencil from time to time when I see a tutee struggling with a problem. It's tough to break this habit. But imagine the xx - yy problem mentioned earlier. Had I watched the tutee work out the problem x = 6 and y = 5, I would have immediately observed that there was a problem.

Work At Your Tutee's Level

When I was working on my Master's degree in mathematics, I attended a class in "Numerical Methods for Solving Partial Differential Equations." The title alone was enough to make me nervous. This was the kind of class that you hoped would be taught by a soft-spoken, patient, and understanding professor. Instead, we got a short-tempered professor who happened to be a leading expert in the field. This guy was so far out there that he couldn't explain things at a level the class could understand.

His way of explaining a problem, when asked by the class, was to repeat word for word what he had previously said...but much louder. Of course, if we didn't get it the first time, we weren't going to get it with this type of explanation. When asked to clarify the problem a little, he would do the same thing again...LOUDER! We quit asking when his voice got too loud to tolerate. It was obvious that this professor, though gifted in his field, could not think or explain things at our level of understanding.

When I was working with my tutee on the xx - yy problem (mentioned above), I was not thinking at my tutee's level of understanding. I knew that implied multiplication exists between variables.

In my mind, this was a basic math concept. Therefore, I did not even consider the possibility that my tutee might not have known this rule.

Assess your tutees' knowledge level by constantly observing their work and progress during the session. Also, use the questioning and listening skills discussed previously.

Don't ever assume your tutee knows something just because you do!

Tutee Summaries And Demonstrations

Imagine a class in mountain climbing. The instructor has broken the subject matter down into several manageable parts. The class learns about choosing the proper clothing for the climb, the gear involved in mountain climbing, and the different types of knots needed for a successful climb. Finally, the time has come for the class to climb a real mountain. Unfortunately, the instructor failed to let the students demonstrate their skills in class, prior to the climb.

One by one, as their knots fail, the students tumble down the side of the mountain.

The instructor made the mistake of moving on with the session even though the students were not prepared to do so.

Back to my tutee and the xx - yy problem. Had I let my tutee summarize the steps to solving this problem or actually demonstrate the steps needed to solve it, I would have immediately noticed that it was not yet time to move on in our session. Summaries and demonstrations by your tutees provide an excellent way for you to assess how much your tutee has mastered.

Never move ahead in a session until your tutee has fully understood the process on which you are working and has developed the skills necessary to carry out the procedure.

Chapter 9

Stellar Student Behavior

Good study skills are contagious!

Your academic habits, whether good or bad, can have a significant impact on your tutee. So, improving (or maintaining) your own study skills is an excellent way to improve the skills of your tutees.

Good Student Behavior

As a good student (that's generally one of the requirements for becoming a tutor) you should be exhibiting good study habits and good student behavior. Your tutee will learn just by observing your actions during a session. A significant amount of learning during a session takes place indirectly, through observation. If you are neat and organized, it may influence your tutee. The act of using a reference book or index can teach your tutee new ways of obtaining information. Using the vocabulary of the subject will help the tutee become more familiar with the subject by learning new words and phrases. How you approach a problem may also give your tutee a new view on problem solving. Also, your interest and enthusiasm for the subject might help an uninterested tutee's motivation.

In addition to what you say and do, pay attention to what your tutee says and does. Your tutee may indicate, usually indirectly, that he or she needs help with a particular study skill. In such cases, the study skill needs to be discussed during your session together. Good study skills are extremely valuable tools, yet most students are lacking in them. Study skill techniques are easy to present, but due to existing habits, these techniques are often difficult to put into practice. Even though you, as a tutor, cannot force your tutees to adopt good study habits, you can stress their importance, show your tutee how to develop them, and encourage their frequent usage.

When addressing study skills, you should not just present the material and move on. You need to hold your tutee accountable for the new skill. The following story illustrates this point.

> **Key Concepts!**
>
> - Look for and address weak study skills
> - Hold the tutee accountable for new skills learned
> - If you can't do a problem, admit it, then turn the situation into a positive one

Suppose your doctor announces that your cholesterol level is 280 (which is too high). You have a serious health problem, but rather than addressing it, your doctor bids you farewell until next year's check up. Now let's suppose that your doctor is a little more conscientious and alert.

After announcing how high your cholesterol level is, your doctor tells you that 280 is too high, and that you must eat a more healthful diet. Are you really going to change your diet just because you doctor told you that you should? Doubtful.

Now suppose that you doctor is REALLY alert. After a discussion about high cholesterol, he or she gives you some very specific instructions for altering your diet, and implementing an exercise regimen. In addition, you are instructed to come back in three months so that your progress can be monitored. Not only has your doctor emphasized the importance of lowering you cholesterol and shown you ways to accomplish this, but he or she has also made you accountable for lowering your cholesterol by asking you to come back for a check up in three months. Whether you choose to follow the doctor's instructions is ultimately up to you. Your doctor can't force you to follow the advice. But chances are, with that much knowledge and accountability, you are going to be much more likely to follow the medical advice.

As a tutor training guide (and not a study skills manual), this book only scratches the surface of good student behavior. There is enough information in this chapter to get you through situations you may encounter during a session. For interested tutors, there are literally hundreds of books available on study skills and techniques. I encourage those of you who are interested (and even those of you who are not!) to read more about study skills. Not only will further reading in this area strengthen your tutoring abilities, but it will also make you a better prepared student.

Help! I Can't Solve This!

Your tutee presents you with
a problem that you can't solve.

Don't panic!

It's okay not to know every answer to every problem. Just be honest. Inform the tutee that you don't have an answer. This will show the tutee that it's okay not to always have an answer.

But don't stop there!

A good tutor will find the answer. If time permits, consult another student, or even another textbook to get the correct answer. Again, your tutee will see that it is okay to consult with other people and resources under these circumstances. It is possible that the answer can be discovered with a little research.

Get the tutee involved!

If more research or time is needed, move on to another problem. Then, if appropriate, challenge your tutee to do some work or research on the problem and present his or her work at your next session. Of course you will want to solve the problem prior to your next session. If necessary, contact the instructor for assistance.

Notetaking

Your tutee repeatedly shows up at your sessions with a book and some paper to write on - but that is all he or she brings.

Your first question should be,
"Where are your notes?"

Many students don't take notes. There are a variety of reasons (also known as excuses!). "The teacher lectures right out of the book." "Notes are a waste of paper and time." "I've never taken notes." Whatever the excuse, you should introduce the tutee to the importance of notetaking and notetaking techniques. In addition, make sure that your tutee knows that he or she is accountable for notetaking. A good idea would be to ask your tutee to bring his or her notes from class to your next session. This will not only help the tutee become responsible for taking notes, but it will also give you the opportunity to assess your tutee's notetaking skills.

> **Exercise**
>
> ***Stumped***
>
> Your tutee presents you with a problem that has you stumped. What should you do?

Consider the importance of notetaking, for example, when you are asking for directions. After asking how to get somewhere, you are given five different street names, four turns (some right, some left), a landmark to watch for, and finally, an address. It is too much information to remember, so you write it down. Maybe you don't like written directions, so you draw a map. And maybe "go north" makes more sense to you than "turn left." The point is that you put the information in your own words, and organize it in a way that makes it understandable to you.

Notes are valuable for a variety of reasons. In a lecture, notes may be your only record of the information presented. By writing something down, especially in your own words, it becomes more understandable. By organizing your notes, material can be presented in a way that makes sense to you. Materials from lectures and your text can be combined in your notes to add more meaning to both.

Notes are also an excellent study guide.

Use summary phrases and questions in your note margins as study aids. While studying, cover your notes, read a phrase or question in the margin, and try to remember the entire item. This is especially helpful preparation for essay exams.

You may also cover the margins, read your notes, and try to summarize them in phrases or questions in the margins. This is especially effective when you are preparing for multiple choice tests.

Here are some good notetaking techniques:

Keep notes together in a notebook, organized by subject/class

Use 8 1/2 x 11 lined, white paper

Put class, title, date, and any other relevant information at the top of each page of notes

Write neatly, and don't crowd

Put one idea on each line

Only capture main points and supporting details. Don't write down everything!

Use your own words

Use abbreviations and shorthand that you can easily understand

Use margins for summaries (phrase or question format) of your notes

Organize your notes in a way that is meaningful to you

Text-Marking

Your tutee is hoping to be paid the maximum price for a textbook because it doesn't have any marks in it! When you see an unmarked book (except in the case of elementary or secondary students who are not allowed to mark in their textbooks), you should introduce your tutee to the importance of text marking, and how to properly mark a text. Again, challenge your tutee to bring a properly marked-up textbook to your next session.

How many times have you read some interesting information in a magazine, and then when you went back to search for it, you could not find it. You were pretty sure where it was, but you just could not locate it. Finally, after skimming over the same few pages four or five times, you found it. It was annoying, not to mention a waste of your time. Now, imagine if you had highlighted the information with a yellow marker.

Text-marking is a valuable tool. It makes important information easy to locate and review. Text-marking also makes you read your text and think about which information is important. Like notetaking, a properly marked text should contain summaries in the margins. In addition, you can use margins to flag examples and definitions you feel are important. Some suggestions for text-marking are listed below:

Use a marker designed for highlighting text

Read the entire section before doing any marking

Mark only important topics and information. Don't mark up the entire book!

Use margins for summaries and questions and to flag definitions and examples

Test Taking

Your tutee complains about performing poorly on tests. After informing your tutee that this is not an unusual problem, introduce the topic of test preparation strategies. Many students don't realize that there are different ways to study for different types of tests. Some preparation strategies are listed below:

Find out about the exam
(type of questions, grading, topics covered, etc.)

Prepare in advance -
don't wait until the last minute!

Arrive on time (not too early, not too late)

Bring all of the necessary materials to the test

Get instructions before you begin the test...
If you're not sure about something - ASK!

Read the questions carefully

Answer the easiest questions first

Guess (if there is no penalty for guessing)

Don't worry about other students
finishing before you:
The only thing you need to concentrate
on is your test

For multiple choice, short-answer, and true or false tests:

Learn themes and ideas - the overall structure of the material

Turn main points into questions

Know terms and vocabulary

Absolute or categorical statements are usually false

Generalizations are usually only partly true

When unsure, eliminate the obvious wrong answers before guessing

For essay style tests:

Identify trends and themes in your material

Organize and restate ideas in your own words

Study discussion questions at the ends of the chapters

Review interrelated information

Write some practice essays on appropriate topics

Read the essay question(s) for a topic (or topics)

Look for words such as causes and results. They direct or restrict your answer

Look for words such as compare,
evaluate, and analyze:
They indicate the kind of information
to include in your answer

Include only one major point per paragraph

Use the paragraph to support the major point

Be direct!
Don't ramble on

Write neatly and use correct grammar and
punctuation

Memorization

Your tutee complains about not being able to remember things during a test. Ask your tutee if he or she remembers the names and phone numbers of friends. Ask your tutee if he or she has forgotten how to drive a car or ride a bike. Point out that he or she can and does remember information. Then emphasize the importance of a good study environment and suggest some techniques for memorizing new material. You might make your tutee accountable by asking him or her to make up vocabulary cards and bring them to your next session.

Have you ever attended a professional conference? The first thing the staff does is give you a name tag. Why bother with the hassle and expense of name tags? After all, when you meet someone at a conference you usually introduce yourselves. The reason is memory. Most of us cannot remember a person's name after one quick introduction, especially when there are so many new people around. But the name tags help us associate names with faces. It's amazing how quickly the name tags help us remember people's names at one of these functions.

To succeed in a subject, you need to memorize certain facts and concepts. There are techniques that you can use to help you memorize facts, but there are also study techniques that will make you more receptive to memorizing information. Some suggestions for improving memory are listed below:

Study in good light, with no distractions, and where it is quiet

Choose a comfortable chair and a table that will accommodate your study materials

Study in the same place each time (if possible)

Study during your "on" time (i.e. "night people" should study at night)

Use frequent, short study sessions (45 minutes/ 10 minute break, as an example)

Associate new material with an interest, hobby, or something you already know

Relate the new material to a strong visual image

Relate information to a humorous or emotional story

Use acronyms or rhymes (Columbus sailed the ocean blue in 1492)

Bring meaning to unclear concepts, it's easier to remember meaningful information

Use 3 x 5 cards - words, math problems or other types of "key" information on one side, definitions or answers on the other side

Time Management

If your tutee constantly complains about not having enough time to complete assignments, you will need to discuss time managment skills.

Even though we all have the same 24 hours in a day, why is it that some people can be the president of three clubs, a member of a sports team, run for a school office, and carry a full class load while the rest of use are doing well to get our homework in on time? Part of the reason is time management. Everyone has certain things that they would like to accomplish in life. Often, old habits and our own personalities get in the way and prevent us from achieving our goals.

Time management is difficult to implement. It requires you to take a good look at how you currently live, and then make changes in your life that will help you achieve your goals. Time management begins with a record of how you spend your time; what do you do each week, and how much time do you spend doing it? Next, goals need to be set. What do you want to accomplish? Goals need to be reasonable and attainable. Once you have reasons (goals) for needing more time, you will be more eager to use your time wisely. Next, priorities should be set. Make a list of all your activities and rank them according to importance. Identify your best (on) and worst (off) times.

Create a master schedule (an entire semester or quarter). This will help you identify your busy and slow times. Next, build a weekly schedule. Begin with fixed activities, such as classes, work, meetings, etc., and include any due dates and estimated study time. Plan separate study times for each class. Try to schedule study times right before or after class meetings. Schedule your most difficult subjects when you are most alert (your "on" times). Don't schedule study sessions that are too long. An hour or less is best. Leave some unscheduled time each day for a "shock absorber."

Once you have developed a schedule, you will probably need to change some personal habits to make it work. This can be the most difficult part of a successful time management program. Don't try to change everything at once, and don't expect miracles of yourself. Modify one behavior at a time. Get help from a friend. Tell your friend what you are trying to do and ask him or her to check with you on a regular (daily is best) basis to assess your progress. Reward yourself for any changes made and goals accomplished. Remember that time management is an ongoing process, so continually assess your progress and set new goals for additional tasks.

Time management can make the difference between having the time to accomplish something or having to settle for second best. A good time management program should include the following:

Set reasonable goals

Set short term goals to allow plenty of time to finish everything

Write down your goals and review them regularly

Use a daily/weekly schedule to keep a prioritized "to do" list

Break large tasks into smaller increments

Schedule important tasks during your "on" time

Do the most important tasks first

Get rid of unnecessary tasks

Group tasks together, when possible

Utilize networking to find study partners

Study in small groups with people you get along with

Share or trade tasks with others

Utilize the internet for research projects

Use e-mail to communicate with your study partners

Check out news groups for help

Learn to use software that can make your assignments a little easier, a lot quicker, and will allow you to prepare professional looking reports and essays

Be productive, efficient, and effective
Don't just keep busy!

Make the most of your time

Learn to say "No" to the things that will interfere with your goals

Keep up a winning, positive attitude

Surround yourself with successful people

Challenge yourself

Cross off tasks that you have completed

Exercise

The Unprepared Tutee

Your tutee consistently comes to sessions unprepared. She hasn't read assignments, doesn't bring her textbook, has no class notes... How would you start this session?

Chapter 10

Potential Problems

Why do so many people learn CPR? After all, when is the last time you ran across someone in need of artificial respiration or a heart massage? For most of us the answer is "never." A statement like, "I'm really glad I know CRP, I just hope I'll never have to use it," is not uncommon among CPR students. So why go to all of the effort to learn something you will probably never have to use? The answer is obvious. If by chance that someone does need CPR, you will be prepared. It's a life-or-death situation. When the time comes, you must be ready to go! If you're not prepared, it's too late.

Although tutoring is not a life-or-death situation (though many students facing an F in a class will tell you otherwise), being prepared in advance for some of the more "uncommon tutoring problems" will allow you to confidently and effectively deal with them, should they arise.

Problems Starting Out

"Man, you're not gonna believe why I was late getting here..."

"I don't mean to be so upset, but I just found out..."

Tutee problems at the beginning of a tutoring session can range from excuses for being late to serious problems requiring professional help. Whatever the case, the problem must be dealt with before effective tutoring can begin. Below are some suggestions for dealing with a variety of tutee problems.

Non-Serious Problems

A non-serious problem is one that can be dealt with quickly and then put aside during the tutoring session. When dealing with a non-serious problem, such as "sorry I'm late, but..." or "I'm really ticked off at the records office because..." it's best to let your tutee talk. Often people need to say something out loud and "get it off their chest". Let your tutee do so. In addition, people in these circumstances need to know that they were heard. Let your tutee know that you were listening by

> **Key Concepts!**
>
> - Avoid unproductive arguments with your tutee
> - Be prepared in advance to handle problems
> - Don't continue the tutoring session if there are problems

verbally acknowledging your tutee's situation. But do not get too involved in the problem. By following these steps, you can avoid adding thoughts of your own that might irritate your tutee or drag you both into an undesirable discussion.

As an example, your tutee rushes into the session late and announces, "My boyfriend is an idiot. First he borrowed my bike without asking, then he got a flat tire and didn't tell me. I found out when I tried to ride over here. I wound up running instead." Your own thoughts on the matter might be something like "It's not that far from your room. You still could have made it on time," or "Why don't you lay down the law with your boyfriend when it comes to your personal property." Either one of these bombshells is likely to upset your tutee or lead to an unproductive discussion. A summarized response of what was said, such as, "I'm sorry you had such a tough time getting over here, but I'm glad you made it. Now let's see, last week we were..." might be a more

Exercise

Habitually late tutees

Your tutee has just arrived 15 minutes late with a poor excuse. This is the third week in a row that this has happened. How would you start the session?

appropriate response. You've acknowledged your tutee and moved on without becoming involved in the tutee's problem.

Of course, there are exceptions. Suppose this is the third or fourth time that your tutee has come up with an excuse for being late. Don't make the tutee feel guilty, don't assign blame, don't discuss how the tutee should run his or her life, and don't make assumptions. Find out why the tutee is repeatedly late. Maybe it's just a simple matter of setting up a new tutoring schedule. If the tutee is always late for no logical reason, review your rules that relate to tardiness. Finally, on rare occasions, you may be required to drop your tutee. After all, if your tutee is unwilling, or unable, to make a reasonable effort, your tutoring efforts will be wasted.

Serious Problems

A serious problem is one that cannot be adequately dealt with and put aside during the session. These could be marital problems, intoxication, traumatic news, etc. Problems of this magnitude will preoccupy your tutee to the point where he or she is not able to concentrate. In such cases, the session should be canceled. Depending on the problem, the session may be rescheduled for a time when the tutee will be able to resume tutoring. In extreme cases, a referral to a professional agency may be required. Don't assume anything. Talk to the tutee and determine if there is a serious problem. If there is a problem, get enough information to make an appropriate referral.

Suppose you are tutoring a tutee in psychology. While reading a paper with your tutee, you discover that he or she was sexually assaulted. Psychological services immediately pops into your mind. Before rushing in with a referral and making a fool of yourself, you wisely decide to ask your tutee for more information. After a short question and answer session, you discover that your tutee has already received counseling and has recovered from the experience. In this case it was a false alarm. The next time, however, it may be real. Only communication with your tutee will reveal if the problem warrants a referral. Some suggestions for making a referral are presented below:

Refer the tutee to a professional that can help.

Be specific in your referral:
Who is the professional?
What are his or her qualifications?
Is there any cost (no cost)?
Who is the contact person/phone number?
Are their services discreet?

Exercise

The Complaining Tutee

Upon his arrival, your tutee begins complaining bitterly about the fact that his girlfriend went out with another guy. How would you handle this tutee?

You should have this information available at all times. If you work in a tutoring center on a school campus, your supervisor should be able to provide you with a list of on-campus referral agencies. When in doubt about a referral, you can always consult with your supervisor. Ultimately, it's your tutee who must decide to seek help. You should, however, be prepared to provide any assistance your tutee may need. This assistance could range from making a phone call to actually escorting your tutee to a facility. You should also continue to show your concern by following up on the referral's outcome. If you had discontinued the tutoring, find out when your tutee might be ready to resume tutoring.

It's a good idea to keep a list of referral agencies on hand. Keep the list up to date and add to it when you discover new referral ideas.

The Health Center, Counseling and Psychological Services, Disabled Student Services, Re-entry Program, and certain clubs on campus are some of the agencies whose services you should be familiar with.

Tutees In Over Their Heads

Occasionally, you may run across a tutee who should not be taking a particular course. Be it lack of a prerequisite or some other fundamental skill, the tutee is not properly prepared for the course. Be honest with the tutee. Suggest that he or she consider taking a prerequisite course or enrolling in a more appropriate course. The tutee might decide to tough it out and continue on with the class. In such cases you have a couple of options. You can either continue tutoring or stop tutoring, depending on the circumstances. The two real-life examples below illustrate both cases.

Bob, a chemistry tutor, was tutoring Janet in chemistry. The course was too advanced for Janet. After their first session, Bob knew that Janet did not have the necessary math skills to succeed in this chemistry class. Bob suggested that she take a refresher course, then try the chemistry. Janet really wanted the chemistry class, so she decided against a refresher course. Instead, she made a serious effort to improve her math skills through tutoring. Because she knew she was at risk, and had committed herself to improving her math skills, Bob decided to continue tutoring her in both math and chemistry. As it turned out, Janet was able to pass the class.

Elizabeth, a business tutor, was tutoring Rick in accounting. Rick had barely passed

Exercise

Doesn't Have What It Takes

It is clear after your second tutoring session that the tutee is lacking the prerequisite knowledge necessary to master the subject. What should you do during your next session?

through the previous accounting class with a "D". After a few sessions, it was obvious that Rick was lacking the fundamentals necessary to survive in the current accounting class. Furthermore, he would show up to sessions unprepared. Elizabeth recommended that he get serious about tutoring or risk failing the course. He insisted on continuing. A few sessions later, Elizabeth dropped him. Because of his lack of knowledge of accounting fundamentals and lack of commitment to the sessions, Elizabeth decided that it was a waste of both his time and hers to continue the sessions.

As a tutor you have the knowledge to spot potential problems like the ones described above. It is your responsibility to asses the situation and suggest any possible alternatives. It is ultimately the tutee's decision as to what course of action he or she will follow.

Chapter 11

I Don't Have To Take This!

Handling Problems

Besides psychological and physical abuse, tutor abuse could also include a repeated disregard for your tutoring rules, a total lack of interest during tutoring, constantly being unprepared for sessions, or any other behavior that disrupts your tutoring efforts. If you are tutoring privately, you need to deal with your tutee directly. Voice your concerns, review your tutoring rules (if applicable), and request that the abuse stop. If it continues, drop your tutee. If you are tutoring at a center you have two options. Depending on the problem, you can either deal directly with your tutee, or take the problem to a staff member in the center. As a third party, a staff member can handle problems in a discrete manner that can keep you separate from the problem. As an example, suppose your tutee has body odor. Not just slight B.O., but major **B.O.** You could talk to your tutee about the situation, but you feel that you and your tutee would be too embarrassed by such a discussion. Instead you mention the problem to an appropriate staff member. The staff member handles the situation by mentioning that the problem has been noticed in the center by various people, thus keeping you out of it. As a staff member and not a peer, the problem can be dealt with in a way that will encourage the tutee to correct the problem without being concerned about other students knowing about it. This is a more discrete approach. In certain circumstances, such as personality conflicts, your tutee might be assigned to a new tutor. In extreme cases, such as sexual harassment, your tutee might be dropped from the tutoring program.

Ultimately, you must decide if you will handle a problem directly, or indirectly, with the help of a staff member. The type of problem, your personalities, and your relationship with your tutee will determine which route you choose.

Tutees Who Insist You Do Their Work

This is not an uncommon problem. Here is a typical scenario: Your tutee arrives with a long homework assignment that is due the next day. As the session begins, your tutee whips out the assignment and insists that the two of you work the problems during the session. When you suggest working a few similar problems (not on the assignment) to demonstrate the process for solving these problems, your tutee gets agitated and impatient.

The tutee in the above scenario is desperate to get the assignment done. But no matter how insistent the tutee might be, it is not the tutor's job to provide a homework service. Once again, doing your tutee's work doesn't teach him or her how to do the work independently. Your tutee might feel like you've been a big help and you

> ## Exercise
>
> ### *Homework Service*
>
> Your tutee arrives for tutoring with a page of 10 homework problems due the next day. He or she insists on doing these problems. How would you conduct this session?

might be happy about your tutee getting the assignment done on time. But what happens when the tutee's instructor gives an exam in class? Are you going to be there to "help out"? And what about the reputation of a tutor or tutoring center that helps students do their homework and other assignments. Instructors want students to do their own work; that is why they assigned it in the first place. A parent paying to have their child tutored wants results for their money. They want their child to learn new skills and processes. They don't want to pay to have their child watch someone else do their assignments. Consistently doing your tutee's homework will lead to a bad reputation as a tutor.

When a tutee persists, explain that you are not a homework service. Most tutoring centers go out of their way to make it clear that their tutors must not do their tutees' homework. If this situation does occur, explain the process and steps required to solve the problems. Then present the tutee with a similar problem to solve. You might let the tutee try one of his or her homework problems (independently) near the end of the session. If the problem continues, you might want to discuss study skills, particularly time management, with the tutee. If the tutee continues to insist that you do the homework, you may end the session and ask that the tutee go off and complete the assignment on his or her own.

One exception is a tutor and tutee going over a term paper. Here, the tutee has already done the work and might be seeking assistance with grammar and punctuation. One idea is to discuss a particular rule and then have the tutee locate and correct these problems in the paper.

Tutees Who Ask You Out

This is one of the most common of uncommon tutoring problems. This problem is often considered tutor abuse, and can be handled using the techniques discussed above. There are rare occasions, however, when a tutor would like to go out with the tutee. If you do choose to go out with your tutee, particularly on a regular basis, it's a good idea to have your tutee assigned to another tutor. Likewise, when private tutoring, you may want to end your tutor/tutee relationship if you begin dating your tutee. Ultimately, the decision is yours and your tutee's, but generally speaking, it's not a good idea to mix business with pleasure.

Chapter 12

That's A Wrap

Ending A Session

Suppose you're in an exercise class. The instructor has chosen a perfect room (environment) for exercising. The instructor also introduced herself at the beginning of the session. In addition, everyone who showed up for the class was given a list of rules to be followed. During the session, the instructor demonstrated new exercises and then watched while the class performed them. Anyone having trouble with the exercise got additional assistance from the instructor. Once an exercise was mastered, a new one was introduced. So far, it sounds like a well-run session. Then, the clock strikes 7 pm and

Key Concepts!

- Assess your tutee's grasp of the big picture
- Give praise for a job well done.
- Keep the tutee active between sessions
- Plan for your next session together

the class is over. The instructor turns out the lights, opens the door, and leaves. What started out as a great session ended in confusion.

What about some cool-off exercises? Should we do any exercises on our own during the week? Do we meet at the same time and place next week? What will we be doing the next time we meet? Like the exercise class above, a tutoring session needs to be ended properly. An appropriate ending to a tutoring session should assess learning, challenge a tutee, and plan for a future session. Some techniques for properly ending a tutoring session are discussed below.

Summarize and Demonstrate

Wait a minute. You might wonder why your tutee should summarize at the end of the session if he or she has already been summarizing throughout the session? There are a couple of reasons. First, having your tutee summarize at the end of the session lets you assess your tutee's understanding of how the newly acquired knowledge fits together and relates to previous knowledge.

For example, suppose you discuss verbs, adverbs, nouns, and pronouns. Your tutee has summarized each of these concepts separately during the session, but does he or she know how to use these forms together in a sentence? Let your tutee summarize the entire session by demonstrating how the items you covered in the session relate to one another or work together. Another reason for a final summary is to reinforce learning. Summarizing at the end of a session gives your tutee an opportunity to review all of what he or she has learned while it is still fresh. Whether your tutee uses a verbal or written demonstration, the act of presenting the material in his or her own words (or actions) will help your tutee to better remember the material. Also, your tutee's summary or demonstration of the session will help you to determine if it is time to move on or if additional work needs to be done.

Praise Your Tutee

Watch a parent when his or her child presents a painting or drawing that they created at school. It doesn't matter how good or bad the artwork is, the child is praised and the work is proudly displayed on the refrigerator door. A young child is one thing, but most of you will be tutoring older people, possibly even adults. It doesn't matter. Believe it or not, even adults enjoy a little praise for a job well done. Praise not only increases your tutees' confidence, but it also lets them know how they are progressing with the material. Keep the praise short and sweet:

You really understand how to...
or
Great job with those...

The praise will vary with each tutee, but don't go hog-wild with praise. Too much praise will waste time, might embarrass your tutee, and could make future praise seem bogus.

Encourage Your Tutee

If you intend to work again with your tutee, you should encourage or challenge your tutee to continue the learning process outside the tutoring session. There are many ways to accomplish this. If a particular problem was unresolved or extremely difficult during the session, you might have your tutee do some work in that area and present findings during the next session. Often it is a good idea to have your tutee read ahead for the next session. Whatever you do, make the tutee responsible for the work. "Bring some ideas on how to solve..." might make your tutee more likely to prepare before the next session than, "Read the section on solving..."

Plan for the Next Session

There's no time like the present! This saying certainly applies to planning for your next tutoring session. Why try to connect during the week to set up an appointment when you can do it right there, in person, at the end of your present session. It makes sense to set up your next tutoring session before your tutee leaves. In addition, plan for any special materials that your tutee might need to bring to the next session.

Good-Byes

Good-bye. We say it at the airport, we say it just before we hang up the phone, we say it when we leave a party, and, yes, we say it at the end of a tutoring session. It's polite and it's professional, and it's really all that needs to be said.

Exercise

Wrap It Up

The tutoring session is nearly over. It went very well. Your tutee seems to have understood all of the concepts covered in the past hour. How will you end this session?

Conclusion

There is more than one "right way" to tutor, and there are plenty of "wrong ways" as well. Many of the "wrong ways" of tutoring presented in the preceding material can be avoided by implementing a little common sense. Nonetheless many tutors, both new and experienced, continue to tutor in the wrong way. Constantly evaluate your skills as a tutor and avoid the "wrong ways" of tutoring. As for the "right ways" of tutoring, some suggestions have been presented in this book. In addition to these, anything you do as a tutor that gets positive results is a "right way" of tutoring. Be creative. What works with one tutee may not work with another. Don't be afraid to try new ways of presenting skills, processes, or material. Also, don't be afraid to abandon an idea that isn't working and move on to another.

Communication with your tutee is important, but so is communication with other tutors. Talk with other tutors, if possible, and find out what works for them. I have personally learned many helpful tutoring techniques from other tutors. When communicating with your tutees be sensitive to their need for self-esteem. An important responsibility of a tutor is to make tutees feel comfortable and confident. A tutee who feels looked down upon, or inferior, will have a difficult time contributing to a tutoring session, whereas a self-confident tutee will be more likely to speak out and participate in the session. Keep in mind that your tutee is not at your level of understanding, and that is to be expected.

Encouragement, patience, and praise can help your tutees' self-esteem. Remember that we all need help sooner or later. And when I need help, I'd rather be helped by a patient and understanding person.

From time to time, think about what you are doing in a session. Are you dominating the session? Who's doing all the talking? Who's doing the work? If you can get your tutee actively involved, if you can employ the techniques discussed above, you will become a more successful tutor.

Finally, if you avoid the "wrongs" and do the "rights", you will be on your way to actually producing an independent learner. And the goal of a tutor should be to enable the tutee to eventually become independent of the tutor.

Practice Makes Perfect

One way to build confidence and prepare for 'real' tutoring sessions is to practice through role-playing. Below are some role-playing ideas to help you practice your skills as a tutor. If you are unable to role-play with another person, try practicing each scenario on your own.

1. Greet a tutee you've never worked with before.

2. Your tutee's last class runs late. As a result, your tutee arrives late and is bitterly complaining about instructors who are not sensitive to students' schedules. Greet this tutee and smoothly transition to tutoring.

3. Your tutee just had a death in the family. He or she begins to cry during your greeting. Determine if a referral is necessary and properly end the session.

4. A returning tutee has arrived late for the third time! Find out what could be done to stop this behavior.

5. For the second time in a row, your tutee arrives wearing a very offensive shirt. Handle this situation in a discrete manner.

6. "I don't understand any of this stuff," announces your tutee. Transition from this statement to a goal and working agenda for the session. Use a subject you are comfortable with during the role-play.

7. When asked to refer to her notes, your tutee replies, "I don't take notes in this class." Provide the tutee with some note-taking skills and make her accountable for them.

8. Your tutee is upset because he received a C- on his last test. Handle this problem so that the tutoring session can commence.

9. Your tutee is confused about how to solve a problem. Use verbal and written communication to find the area of confusion and corect it.

10. Your tutee presents you with a difficult problem. After a minute or so, it is obvious that you cannot solve it. Turn this into a positive situation and involve the tutee.

11. Role-play a situation demonstrating the importance of having your tutee summarize before moving on to new material.

12. After your second session together, it is obvious that you cannot work well with your tutee (personality conflict, etc.). Handle this situation without offending the tutee.

Index

Give the gift of good tutoring!
Greenwood's Guide For Tutors

YES! I want _____ copies of *Greenwood's Guide For Tutors* for $14.95 (US) each.

Please include $5.95 S&H for one to five books (contiguous states only / FedEx Ground). California residents, please include applicable sales tax. Payment must accompany orders. Please see our website for all other ordering and shipping options.

My check or money order for $______ is enclosed.

Please charge my ☐ Visa ☐ MasterCard

Name ____________________________________

Organization ______________________________

Address __________________________________

City/State/Zip ____________________________

Phone ______________ E-Mail ______________

Card # ___________________________________

Exp. Date _______ Signature _______________

Make your check payable and return to

Dionysus Publishing
3656 Williams Avenue
Claremont, CA 91711

You can also order direct from our website
www.DionysusPublishing.com